*Psittacosaurus mongoliensis* (sit-TAK-oh-SOR-us MON-gol-e-EN-sis) grew up to six and a half feet long and lived from around 113 to 107 million years ago. *Psittacosaurus* was an even more primitive ceratopsian than *Protoceratops*. Its beak reminded scientists of members of the Psittacidae family—that is to say, parrots—so it was given a name meaning parrot (*psittaco*) lizard (*saurus*). *Mongoliensis* refers to Mongolia, the site of the skeleton's discovery.

Pebbles found in the skeleton of one *Psittacosaurus* suggest that this plant eating dinosaur may have swallowed stones to use them as gastroliths, small rocks that help an animal's digestion by grinding food in the stomach.

# DINOSAURS AT THE ENDS OF THE EARTH

Dr. Roy Chapman Andrews
Leader and Zoologist

Walter Granger
Chief Paleontologist
and Second-in-Command

George Olsen
Assistant in Paleontology

Expedition prepares for departure from Peking on April 17, 1922

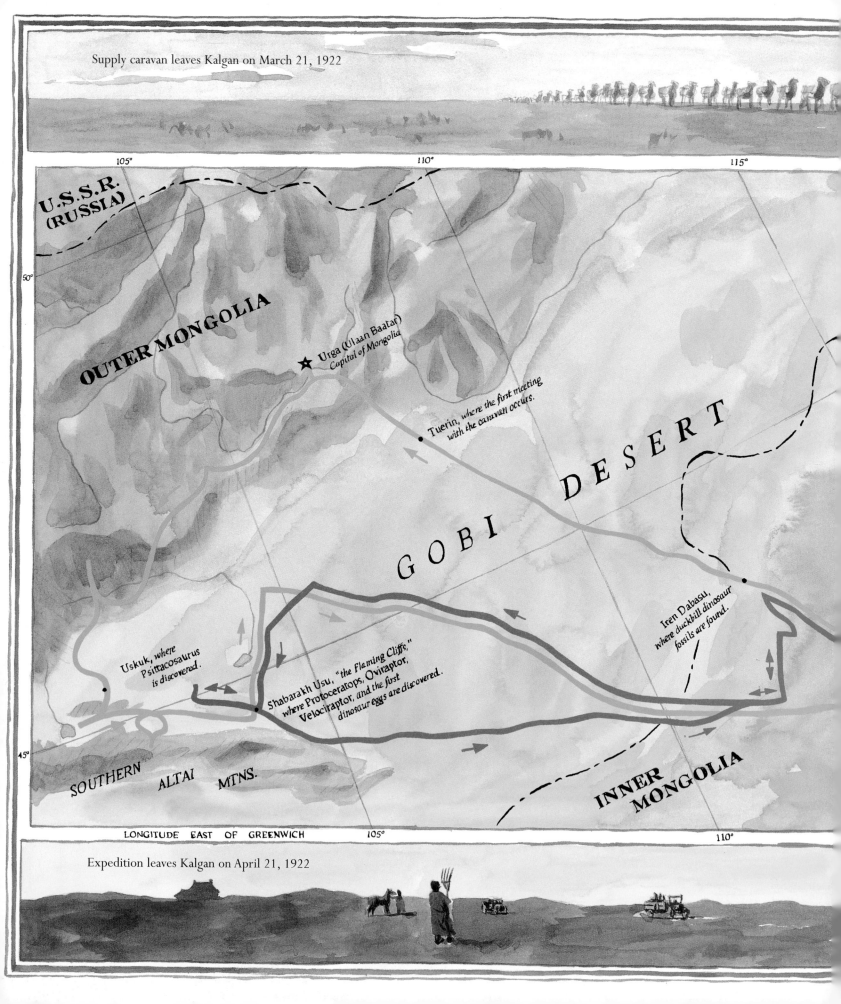

Supply caravan leaves Kalgan on March 21, 1922

105°    110°    115°

U.S.S.R.
(RUSSIA)

50°

OUTER MONGOLIA

★ Urga (Ulaan Baatar)
*Capital of Mongolia*

*Tuerin, where the first meeting*
*with the caravan occurs.*

G O B I   D E S E R T

*Iren Dabasu,*
*where duckbill dinosaur*
*fossils are found.*

*Uskuk, where*
*Psittacosaurus*
*is discovered.*

*Shabarakh Usu, "the Flaming Cliffs,"*
*where Protoceratops, Oviraptor,*
*Velociraptor, and the first*
*dinosaur eggs are discovered.*

45°

SOUTHERN   ALTAI   MTNS.

INNER MONGOLIA

LONGITUDE   EAST   OF   GREENWICH    105°    110°

Expedition leaves Kalgan on April 21, 1922

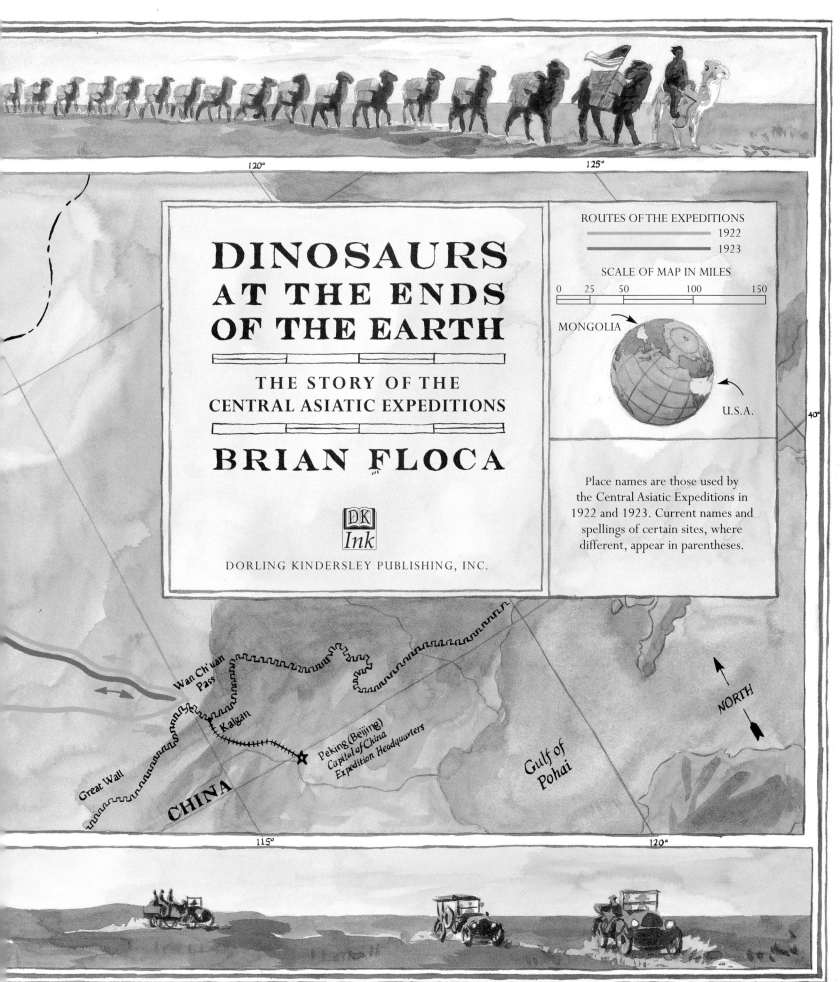

# DINOSAURS AT THE ENDS OF THE EARTH

## THE STORY OF THE CENTRAL ASIATIC EXPEDITIONS

### BRIAN FLOCA

DK Ink

DORLING KINDERSLEY PUBLISHING, INC.

ROUTES OF THE EXPEDITIONS

1922

1923

SCALE OF MAP IN MILES

0    25    50    100    150

MONGOLIA

U.S.A.

Place names are those used by the Central Asiatic Expeditions in 1922 and 1923. Current names and spellings of certain sites, where different, appear in parentheses.

120°

125°

40°

115°

120°

Wan Chi'uan Pass

Kalgan

Great Wall

CHINA

Peking (Beijing)
Capital of China
Expedition Headquarters

Gulf of Pohai

NORTH

*For Greg Street*

For friendly and valuable assistance at the American Museum
of Natural History's Special Collections Library,
the author wishes to thank Flora Rodriguez,
Julie Kasper, and Barbara Mathé.

*A Richard Jackson Book*

Dorling Kindersley Publishing, Inc., 95 Madison Avenue, New York, New York 10016
Visit us on the World Wide Web at http://www.dk.com

Text and illustrations copyright © 2000 by Brian Floca

Dorling Kindersley books are available at special discounts for bulk purchases for sales promotions or premiums. Special editions,
including personalized covers, excerpts of existing guides, and corporate imprints can be created in large quantities
for specific needs. For more information, contact Special Markets Dept., Dorling Kindersley Publishing, Inc.,
95 Madison Avenue, New York, New York 10016; fax (800) 600-9098.

Library of Congress Cataloging-in-Publication Data
Floca, Brian.
Dinosaurs at the ends of the earth: the story of the central Asiatic expeditions / Brian Floca.
p.  cm.
"A DK Ink book."
Summary: Describes the expeditions led by Roy Chapman Andrews for New York's American Museum of Natural History
to the Gobi Desert in Mongolia in an effort to uncover dinosaur fossils.
ISBN 0-7894-2539-4
1. Andrews, Roy Chapman, 1884-1960—Juvenile literature. 2. Naturalists—United States—Biography—Juvenile literature. 3.
Dinosaurs—Eggs—Juvenile literature. 4. Central Asiatic Expeditions (1921-1930)—Juvenile literature. [1. Andrews, Roy Chapman,
1884-1960  2. Naturalists. 3. Paleontologists.] I. Title.
QH31.A55 F57 2000  508'.092—dc21  [B]  99-043071

The illustrations for this book were created with watercolor and gouache.
The text of this book is set in 16 point Perpetua.
Printed and bound in U.S.A.
First Edition, 2000
2  4  6  8  10  9  7  5  3  1

"This is your first trip to Mongolia, isn't that right, George?" asked Roy Chapman Andrews.

"Sir?" George Olsen said. "Yes, sir." He took a look over his shoulder. The farmers watching them from outside the Wan Ch'uan Pass grew smaller and smaller. Not all of them, George had heard, expected the expedition to make it back.

"Dr. Andrews," George asked when the expedition was just beyond the pass, "how exactly did you figure out these motorcars would make it across Mongolia?"

"That's what Dr. Osborn at the museum wanted to know, George," said Andrews. "Back in New York I told him, 'Dr. Osborn, everyone who has tried to explore the Gobi Desert has used camels, but with automobiles we could cover ten times the amount of ground.' And he said to me, 'But, Roy, there are no roads in the Gobi. How do you know automobiles will work out there?'"

"And what did you say, sir?"

"I said, 'I don't *know* it, but I believe it can be done.' Now *push,* boys, push!"

At least overall, George kept telling himself, things are off to a smooth start. Aside from some trouble with the mud here and there, the motorcars made good time, just as Andrews had planned. They sped toward Urga, the Mongolian capital, bouncing like corks on the sea over the stones and ruts of an ancient caravan trail. In the cars rode the some twenty men Andrews had brought together for the Central Asiatic Expeditions: interpreters, cooks, mechanics, and scientists like Walter Granger, for whom George would work as an assistant.

It was their job to find and study fossils.

That night at the campfire the talk turned to what George and Granger might hope to discover.

"Of course, we can't be sure we'll find anything at all," Granger said. "Plenty of people have told me that spending five months out here following Roy around will be a waste of time and talent and money and so on."

"I've been told we'd have better luck looking for fossils on the bottom of the ocean," Andrews said.

Granger continued. "But, scientifically speaking, Central Asia is virtually unknown. As the first scientists to give it a serious look, we've got the potential to discover a great deal."

"It's a gamble," Andrews said. "It will either make all our reputations or ruin mine."

As the expedition approached Iren Dabasu, the grasslands gave way to the fine gravel of the Gobi floor, and the fossil hunting began. George paced back and forth, repeating Granger's instructions. Look for the flash of white, he told himself. Look for the bits that might be bone, uncovered by the constant wind. Granger had already found fragments of bone, duckbill dinosaur, he thought, and occasionally he would call out, "Over here, George! This might be worth a look!" But George, his head bowed hard and his neck aching, was having less luck. His eyes wandered to Andrews and the interpreters, who were stepping into one of the tentlike structures the expedition had come across that morning.

These yurts were the homes of nomadic herdsmen, to whom the Americans and their cars seemed exotic and strange. Inside the yurt, George knew, Andrews hoped to hear news of the expedition's supply caravan. Although a camel caravan was slow, it could still carry more than cars could. This one had been loaded with gasoline, food, and other supplies. A Mongolian named Merin had led it out of China weeks before the expedition began, so that the camels and the cars would arrive together in the desert.

"They passed by here two weeks ago," Andrews said when he emerged. "Right on schedule."

As the expedition approached the old lama monastery near Tuerin, George
saw a massive caravan stretching across the desert. A sun-bleached American
flag told him it was their own. Merin and his seventy-five camels had arrived
just an hour before the cars.

"Like clockwork, George!" Roy said. "Like clockwork."

Expedition members unloaded the supplies they would need until the
next meeting with the caravan and began their work. Often members of the
expedition split into several small camps to pursue their specialties. George
and Granger continued looking for fossils. Other scientists studied the land,
the plants, and the wildlife. Andrews drove ahead as a scout, and when he
returned the expedition pressed forward and began work at the next campsite.
The caravan followed, reaching the new camp by the time the expedition again

needed fresh supplies. These meetings formed the pattern of the expedition and allowed it to stay stocked with gasoline and food as it moved steadily toward Urga and then turned to the southwest, toward the Altai Mountains.

As the cars struggled over the old trails, George could sometimes see men on horseback in the distance, shadowing the expedition with rifle barrels flashing in the sun.

"Bandits, most likely," Andrews said. "Kula, if our luck's run out. Or maybe renegade Mongolian soldiers. Or renegade Chinese soldiers, and we shouldn't rule out the Russian Bolsheviks. Of course, even Czarists are a possibility."

"Well," George finally said, "which should we hope for?"

Granger said, "Hope that you're seeing things."

Near the Altai, at Uskuk, George did see something. He led Granger and Andrews to a series of white flecks in the earth, then hesitated. "I'm not so sure, now that I have another look," he said. The morning light had shifted, and the shapes seemed to have shifted, too. "Maybe they're bone," George said. "But maybe they're just rocks?"

"Maybe," said Andrews, "it's a priceless fossil. I'll get the pickaxes, you two get the shovels, and we'll find out."

Granger winced. "Roy," he said, "if I see you within fifty feet of this spot with a pickax—" Andrews put up his hands, stopping Granger in midsentence. The careful work of digging up fossils was more Granger's skill than his, and he knew it. And if there was something reluctant in Andrews's slow walk back to camp, it earned him no sympathy from Granger. "If Roy had his way," he said, "we'd have this dug up in an hour. It would be smashed to pieces, but we'd have it dug up." The comment reminded George that he had once heard Andrews called the accelerator and Granger the brake.

With that he and Granger lowered themselves to the ground and began to brush away gravel with whisk brooms. A fossil began to show itself, and they switched to delicate camel's-hair brushes. Once the loose dirt was removed, George and Granger chipped gingerly at the matrix, the earth and stone encasing the fossil. Where Andrews might have wielded a pickax, they used finer tools, some as precise as dental instruments. The only sounds as the hours wore on were a methodical scraping and tapping.

By afternoon, the temperature had reached 110 degrees. The horizon shimmered in the distance, and the water in George's canteen felt so hot in his throat he could barely drink it. Rocks bit into his shins and knees, and dirt and sweat stained his shirt. But George did not mind. The flecks of bone had revealed themselves to be part of a tail, and the tail had led to a body, and the body to a skull. "Nice-looking rocks, George," was all Granger said.

As George chipped around the skeleton, something flickered on the horizon. A brown blur marred the sky, like a smudge on a window. Granger followed George's gaze, then cupped his hands around his mouth and turned toward the main camp. "Inside the tents!" he bellowed. "Hold down the tents!" He turned back to George. "Sandstorm."

The storm rushed across the desert, dimmed the sun to a ruddy circle, and then swept it from the sky. In the fading light, George saw other members of the expedition scramble for shelter, but there was no time for him or Granger to get back to camp. The wind was already strong and cool. Sand and dirt were already pricking at his skin. Almost tenderly, Granger spread himself over part of the fossil, shielding it from the coming storm. As a wall of sand thundered toward him, George's eyes ran along the curves of the bones, the tracery of a creature never before imagined. Sand seemed to pour from the sky. George pulled his shirt collar over his face to help him breathe. He bent low over the exposed half of the fossil, next to Granger. Their eyes met only for a moment.

"What I want to know," Granger shouted over the wind, "is who's going to excavate *us*?" Then the storm thickened and each man became invisible to the other. The air howled, whipping gravel that scraped and tore and punched. For a half hour George absorbed the blows, until the winds finally eased and only gentle gusts of sand lapped against torn clothes and skin.

In the clearing air George and Granger coughed, stood, and brushed themselves off. Beneath a mask of dirt, George surprised himself by smiling. The two scientists were as good as wrecked, but the fossil was okay.

Although the fossil was uncovered, the excavation was far from complete. Where the soft bones might crumble, Granger applied a thin coat of gum arabic. With delicate touches, he then pressed on sheets of Japanese rice paper to hold any small fragments in place. Then George dipped strips of burlap in a plaster of flour paste. The strips, heavy and soggy, were laid over the rice paper and the surrounding matrix. By the next afternoon the burlap had hardened into a protective cast, called a jacket. George and Granger began to dig a small trench around and under the fossil, enclosing it on all sides with plaster as they went.

When only a slight pedestal of earth remained beneath the fossil, Granger invited Andrews back to the dig site. Andrews and others joined George and Granger and gripped, carefully and nervously, the edges of the heavy rock. "Easy, easy," Granger pleaded. With a great heave the fossil was lifted and turned over. By evening it was entirely wrapped in plaster. Once that hardened, the fossil was ready for the long trip back to the museum, where it would be uncovered again, cleaned, and studied.

In a sense the museum was where the real work would begin, where careful observations would be made, where theories about the skeleton would be developed and tested, and where this small dinosaur would be given the name *Psittacosaurus*. But even without knowing fully what he had found, George felt the excitement of discovery, felt as if he had found a note or a clue, left just for him, about a world millions of years gone. He felt as if he had gotten a glimpse back in time.

George's and Granger's newly prepared fossil joined others, all jacketed in plaster, carefully labeled, and stacked in the corner of a tent. The stack was growing into a great pile, and nobody worried anymore about the summer being a waste of time. There were so many discoveries that when Merin and the caravan failed to appear at one campsite, the scientists quickly ran out of flour and burlap. To keep working they had to resort to substitutions.

For flour, they simply used the supply they had brought for food. But the burlap was more troublesome. It was not the most inspiring moment of the summer, but when Andrews came by George's tent to say "We're ready for your underwear, George," George handed it over. Strips of underwear, wash-cloths, tent flaps, shirts, and Andrews's pajamas were plastered around fossils before the caravan, delayed by drought, finally arrived.

The scientists eagerly removed the fresh supplies from the camels and in their place loaded the fossils. For extra padding, Andrews wrapped the bones in the heavy wool shed by the camels. George knew that Andrews thought this a clever use for the wool, and overheard him boast, "No finer packing material could be devised." Then he caught Granger mumbling, "Tell that to my underwear."

In early September the expedition reached a gorge the local herdsmen called Shabarakh Usu. Andrews, watching the sunset play on the crags and bluffs, called it the Flaming Cliffs. The site looked promising for fossil hunting, but summer was fading quickly. Rushed by threat of winter, the expedition stayed less than a day.

It was when they returned the next summer that George set off on his own for a walk. He worked his way up the side of the gorge until he could survey the entire area, and craned his head this way and that, wondering where he might find the best sites to dig. He leaned out from the wall of the gorge to improve his view, and then leaned a little farther, until he was so far out that when the soft earth beneath his feet broke into loose clods of dirt, he tumbled forward. His arms flailed and his feet rolled over his head as he slid down the slope in a cloud of sand. George came to a halt, almost too embarrassed to care anymore about dig sites. Almost, but not quite. Something caught his eye.

George rushed to deliver his news to Granger and Andrews back at the mess tent, gasping and grinning as he spoke.

"Eggs?" Andrews said. "Slow down, George. You've found fossilized eggs? You're sure you didn't hit your head when you fell?"

Granger tried to be sympathetic. "I'm sorry," he said. "You know we date that area of the gorge at eighty million years. There were no birds in the Cretaceous Period large enough to lay eggs like the ones you're describing. I'll have a look, but they're probably just odd sandstone formations."

George knew it sounded a little ridiculous. He smiled, though, and said, "Laugh if you want, but these are eggs."

"Could be heatstroke," Andrews said with a grin. Nevertheless, he and Granger climbed into a car with George and headed toward the cliffs. There, beside a small ledge, George pointed out the three shapes. Granger and Andrews tried to think of some explanation other than the obvious one, until finally Andrews broke the silence. "Well," he said, "an egg's an egg."

"They can't be bird eggs. We know that from how old they are," said Granger. "And, anyway, they're not the right shape. They're too elongated, more like reptile eggs." Granger paused. "That leaves only one possibility."

George had an idea of what Granger might be thinking. He loosened one of the eggs and lifted it in his hand. It felt as heavy as a stone, with a pebbled texture to its broken surface. A smile spread across Granger's face. "George Olsen," he said, "you have discovered—you are holding—an egg laid by a dinosaur."

These were the first dinosaur eggs ever found, and of the many discoveries made by the Central Asiatic Expeditions, George Olsen's proved the most spectacular. Newspaper headlines declared it around the world. Scientists could now say with certainty that dinosaurs were not born, but hatched.

"A dinosaur nest! Mr. Olsen," said Roy Chapman Andrews, "congratulations!"

The Flaming Cliffs proved to be one of the richest sites of dinosaur fossils ever found. There *Protoceratops* may have roamed in great herds, grazing slowly while nearby an *Oviraptor* guarded its nest, or thundering away from an attack of *Velociraptor*. In the shadows of these beasts small mammals, distant ancestors of mammals alive today, must have scurried to avoid being crushed.

Those strange animals lay buried and hidden for eighty million years. The discoveries of the Central Asiatic Expeditions, and of the scientists who followed them, allow us to imagine that world before ours, when dinosaurs walked the earth.

*Oviraptor philoceratops*

This timeline shows how scientists divide the history of life on Earth, first into eras, and then into smaller units called periods. For example, knowing that the eggs George Olsen found were eighty million years old, we can say that they were from the Mesozoic Era and, more specifically, the Cretaceous Period.

| PRECAMBRIAN | PERIODS CAMBRIAN | ORDOVICIAN | SILURIAN | DEVONIAN |
|---|---|---|---|---|
| | ERAS PALEOZOIC | | | |

570    550         500         450         400

Millions of years ago

*Velociraptor mongoliensis*      *Protoceratops andrewsi*

| CARBONIFEROUS | PERMIAN | TRIASSIC | JURASSIC | CRETACEOUS | QUARTERNARY → TERTIARY | PRESENT DAY |
|---|---|---|---|---|---|---|
| | | MESOZOIC | | | CENOZOIC | |

350          300          250          200          150          100          50

Dinosaurs appear            Fall of the dinosaurs        Humans appear

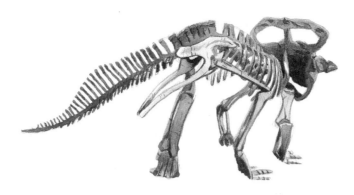

## A Note on the Story

Elements in this story have been imagined or fictionalized, but the Central Asiatic Expeditions and their discoveries were real.

Their leader, Roy Chapman Andrews, was born in 1884 in Beloit, Wisconsin. He moved to New York City in 1906 with the hope of working as a naturalist at the American Museum of Natural History. Told there were no jobs available, he convinced the director to let him mop the floors. He worked his way up, earned his doctorate, and traveled on adventures around the world.

Andrews led the first of the Central Asiatic Expeditions into Mongolia in 1922. Some dubbed them the "Missing Link Expeditions" because Andrews hoped to find evidence of human origins in Asia. The expeditions never did, but what they did discover and collect amazed the world. In 1930, Mongolia was effectively closed to Western scientists, ending Andrews's expeditions. In 1934, he became director of the museum. A less able administrator than explorer, a self-described "square peg in a round hole," he retired in 1941 and devoted himself to his writings. Roy Chapman Andrews died in 1960.

Soviet, Polish, and Mongolian teams continued exploration of the Gobi, and in 1990 the government of Mongolia invited teams from the American Museum of Natural History to return to the sites pioneered by Andrews. At this writing, joint Mongolian and American teams continue to visit the Flaming Cliffs, refining our understanding of old discoveries and making new ones. The work of scientists past and present can be seen at the American Museum of Natural History in New York City and in museums around the world.

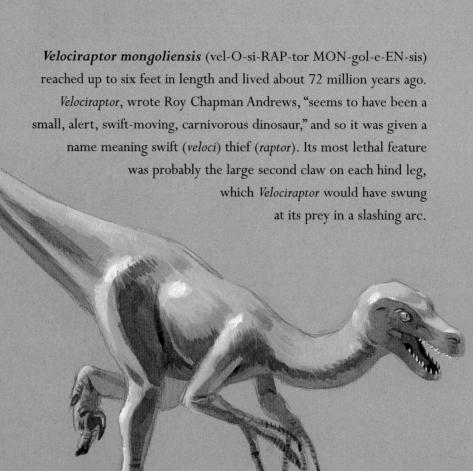

***Velociraptor mongoliensis*** (vel-O-si-RAP-tor MON-gol-e-EN-sis)
reached up to six feet in length and lived about 72 million years ago.
*Velociraptor*, wrote Roy Chapman Andrews, "seems to have been a
small, alert, swift-moving, carnivorous dinosaur," and so it was given a
name meaning swift (*veloci*) thief (*raptor*). Its most lethal feature
was probably the large second claw on each hind leg,
which *Velociraptor* would have swung
at its prey in a slashing arc.

In 1971, a Polish-Mongolian expedition discovered an
extraordinary *Velociraptor* fossil, which lay frozen in struggle
with the skeleton of a *Protoceratops*. The *Velociraptor's* claws
were pulled up toward the *Protoceratops's* throat, and one of its
arms was held fast in the *Protoceratops's* jaws. Perhaps the
struggle exhausted and killed both animals,
or perhaps they were buried together by
a sandstorm as they fought.